Russell

Prison or Passion
Poetry & Prose Collection

by
R.K. Russell

Russell

"To all the women who raise men,
The world isn't aware of how vital you are."

Russell

Table of Contents
The Warden Isn't Home... 4
The Prison Has Flowers... 34
The Free Man Repletion...80

Russell

The Warden Isn't Home

Russell

Here To Stay

The only thing that won't
Leave me
Are these abandonment issues.

Love's Name

I don't know love's name.
I call at it with pronouns. Ma'am. Sir. Hey you.
I wait to make eye contact. To get love's attention and obtain its affection.

I don't know love's name.
I wave in its direction but never touch.
Love never sees me.

I don't know love's name.
Maybe it's because these scars have me too terrified
To introduce myself first.

Neverland

I've always been fascinated with Peter Pan.

His proposal sweetened by pixie dust and dreams that soar like him. Many nights I imagined the timeless boy tapping on my window in twilight. The way questions would fall over each other and tumble out of my mouth. Would he hear them over my grumbling stomach?

You see Peter, I've been a lost boy. I don't need to run away because I was born into abandonment. I knew I had truly found Neverland because they would never love me.

Peter what do you fear? You never age, you'll never die. Peter, I've been dying everyday. Loneliness my silent, slow, deliberate, killer. Surely a boy as hollow and empty as me can fly.

In my Neverland there is no Captain Hook. No one chases after this lost boy. God, I wish someone hated me that much. I wish I made someone feel something.
Damn it Peter, I wish I made anyone feel anything. I stayed up so late imagining what I would say to that timeless boy when he tapped on my window in the
twilight.

Every night came. Every morning followed.
There was never a tap.
Neverland.

Four Letter Word

Don't talk about

F
O
U
R

letter words you don't believe in.

Open Door

I could feel the calluses on his hands as he held my heart.

He turned it over roughly a few times, growing familiar with its fragile surface.
Once he found the chamber where I held my love for him; he impaled the spot with both thumbs.
Gold rushed out and flowed over a bare ring finger and extended all the way to a scarred wrist; a failed attempt at silence.

He continued to peel my heart back turning it inside out, and I watched in self hating amusement.
After he rang the light from every corner he dropped the cold, empty, organ on stone floor and walked out.
I realized he didn't bother closing the door in the first place.
That's a sign that should have told me he wasn't staying long.
I crawled over to the heart, my heart, not knowing I was on the floor the whole time.
For years I sat in that spot.
That one spot, and I filled my heart with love, light, and with GOLD.

After a few years I hear a knock at the door, and I let my father in to repeat a process my mind tells me I deserve.

Piece by Piece

Don't cry to me about how you fell apart.
I was born piece by piece shattered, torn, and broken.
I was never whole.

Face to Face

I pray to God so much
That some day soon
I think we should just talk
Face to face.

Pain is Proof

If pain is the proof that we exist...
My consciousness must live on every plane,
Every dimension... I must have multiple present lives as a
Woman,
as an eagle,
as a star,
as a tree...
I must live deep in the galaxy where comets soar into planets and become nothing more than pain.

Void

He made sure I was empty.
Used his manhood to hollow me out.
Severed my innocence and split my sanity.
I've been trying to fill myself up and sew myself
Together ever since.

Knife to a Gun Fight

My mother was so focused on protecting me
From the stray bullets in the street,
She never thought about
Hiding the razor blades
In the cabinets.

Kids Say

Kids have an uncanny way of making you feel bad about your version of normal.

I didn't know my home was broken until they pointed out the cracks.

Johnny didn't understand why my mother and I didn't share a last name. In elementary school sharing blood didn't seem to be enough. He used all of quiet time
being very vocal about how I could not be her son. I should have known better. I mean I saw first hand the scar that ran from hip to hip. Where they pried me from her belly. The umbilical cord was my first noose and
every time she pushed I hung. It wouldn't be the last noose I tied.

Johnny couldn't understand why I walked home alone from school everyday. In elementary school if the other kids didn't see something, it didn't exist. He thought it strange that my mother didn't pick me up. I explained to him she worked two jobs to provide for me. He used recess time to play with my emotions. He told me she didn't love me. Asked where my father was. I told him I had two. One harder to find than Waldo and the other never moved from the marked grave I visited. It wouldn't be the last grave I visited.

Johnny was irritated that I kept declining his offer to come over. In elementary school it was super important to spend time with your school friends outside of school. I used lunchtime to show him what was eating away at me. This was actually the first fist fight I had in school. I must admit hunger had me irate. It's hard

talking yourself down when you can't hear your subconscious over your rumbling stomach. I swung a punch for everyday that week I came to school with no lunch. I think Johnny was used to taking a hit. Johnny's dad picked him up
everyday, and home seemed like the last place Johnny wanted to go. With more smirk than smile, and rough hands that knew no limits. Maybe Johnny should have come to my house instead. An empty refrigerator was better than an empty heart, and just as cold. I was never going to prod a monster that hid in plain sight. I learned that lesson. It wouldn't be the last time I learned that lesson.

Kids have an uncanny way of making you feel bad about your version of normal.

My definition of normal was synonymous with survival.

Play with Me

She stabbed me
With a joystick
Straight in my chest,
And began to play
With my heart.

Fairytale

Would I even know what my heart looked like if I saw it today? Thick walls rise and fall in maze like pattern, constantly changing around my inner chalice. Who knows what is really located on the highest floor, behind bolted door, of a tower far in Neverland. Is there snow without white? Dark shades of dungeon dragons scorned, scarred, and flaming. I thought I would die young. Born in a place coordinated opposite of any fairy tale.

The ugliest flowers are those at funerals. Think about it. They must be, since I can't remember what they looked like as they laid next to my father's closed eyes. Were there even flowers? My first time seeing a dead body all I could think of was the stillness. I've never seen someone that still. I've never seen him that still. No vulgar words being screamed at a tv screen of sports gladiators.
Lips locked and shut.
No eyes radiantly lit telling me, joy lives deep past any accomplishment or disappointment.
Eyes locked and shut.
When I lay my head on his chest the rise and fall of his lungs.
The steady beat of his heart.
So strong.
So steady.
Now still.
So still.

If Excalibur was a heart could it be pulled from stone? Better yet, would anyone want to try their luck? A sword that promised a

kingdom opposed to a heart that promised, what?
Brokenness. Pain. Confusion.
Who is the fairest of them all? It isn't life. It isn't humanity. What about this world is fair? I'm surrounded by humans with no humanity; bigots with no humility. Close me off. Lock me up. Put me in the highest tower, through the darkest forest, far in a place Jesus hasn't walked.

Is that hell? Is this hell? If solidarity is my punishment I'll take it as reward. If I'm condemned, then I am saved. My
salvation lies in a dungeon untouched by those who feed off of sins like food groups. Let me die here alone with no one to bury me.
Let me lie still.
So still.
Until the worms in the earth move me.
Until birds descend and pick at me, bringing me to flight.
Until seeds take root and flowers bloom through my rib cage.
I am born again.
No longer still.
No longer alone.
Happily ever after.

Overdraw

Gold coins. Dollars. Cents.
Money can't buy me a dad.
Birthday transactions aren't bank statements but hugs and laughs.
Silver dollar. The little boy holler. No father to calm his cries.
Plastic credit card. Cold and hard like the floor you left me to sleep on.
I was below zero. It only takes one number, and plenty commas to make you love a zero.
Should I pay you to love me?

I prayed for you to love me.

I cried for you to love me.

I bled for you to love me.

My deposit insufficient.

Lady Luck

Lost two dads
How unlucky am I?
Lost isn't the right word though.
The first left my life
Around the time I left the womb.
The other wasn't lost but stolen.
Stolen in a motorcycle crash
Before I was old enough to realize
Just how much I would need him.

I see why they call her Lady Luck.
Maybe she has something against men.
I don't blame her.

Answer Me

Why hurt someone whose only intention was to love you?

Sitting Down

Running on two hours of sleep and drunk at brunch, I broke out into hysterical laughter. I chuckled and yelled so loud that I actually brought myself to tears. Tears I couldn't even shed at my grandfather's funeral. He had the type of cancer you don't try and fight. I think life is hard enough without your body eating away at itself. Cancer ate away at his lungs, and circumstance ate away at my faith.

I'm sorry.
What was I telling you?
I was sitting on a ledge in Hollywood Hills gazing down on Sodom & Gomorrah. Two espressos transformed three hours of sleep into an eternity. I was alone; so naturally I felt overwhelmed and crowded. My shadow self
reminding me how pathetic I was in soft gentle
whispers. He never yells at me. I can't tell him to stop because I don't want to be alone. Women so willing to enter my bed but never my heart. I wonder what love feels like? Valentine's Day is always warm candles, red hearts, and roses. It's so in your face vibrant, over the top and in your face. Red. Red. Red. I bet love is blue. Easy like the ocean waves on a clear day. Cool like Venice beach in the morning.
And like the ocean, love would swallow me up whole. I would never be able to see the end of it. I wouldn't have to change or conform it would just hold me perfect. I know love is blue.

Dang.
I keep getting off topic. I need to start sleeping.
Where were we again? I was sitting right? Yes, I'm sitting in a hard metal chair in the middle of Disneyland. Like a

bee hive had just been cracked open, children buzzed and zipped past me at every turn tempted to sting. I tried to scarf down this veggie wrap, but like my heart it was cold and poorly put together. Why does sadness taste so bad when surround by joy? Opposites attract and the pure and innocent were all around me. No one ever loved me like this. My dad wouldn't take me to a dentist let alone a theme park. I don't know my birthstone, but every birthday you missed made me jaded. I don't think I would be here if you would have known 25 years ago that condoms are cheaper than love....

What was I telling you? Never mind I'm just going to go sit down.

Lunacy

I'm losing my mind.
Unlike the way you lose a set of keys.
Closer to losing your appetite.
Nothing will crave the hunger you feel.

I'm losing my mind.
Unlike the way you lose track of time.
Closer to losing a loved one.
Time stolen that you'll never get back.

I'm losing my mind.
Unlike losing your virginity.
Closer to losing your innocence.
Not sure when it happened,
Just knowing you'll never get it back.

The Real You

I wonder what you dreamt about
Before you ever knew failure.
What was your heart's desire
Before you ever let them break it?

Open Book

What's the point of being an
Open book
If no ones willing to read it?

Delphi

There's nothing wrong with loving my brokenness.
Just don't use it to control me,
And don't promise you can fix me.
Let's just lay in my collapse and find love amongst my ruin.

Soft Confessions

I spoke to you softly about my past, more out of warning than confession.
Lies and love tasted the same on the bitter tongue of the scorned.
My heart was broken and torn.
You thought if you fixed it, I'd be your possession.
Happy endings and fairytales through teary eyes became deformed.
To call me baby, was a knife to the throat.
To say I love you was a witch's curse.
The only words I let close to my heart were from the good book's verse.

Hiding in Sight

Every time I show you more of my body
I hide more & more of my soul...
of my heart.

Tequila Shots

I thought that I would find the secret to loving myself,
Written on a note at the bottom of a bottle.
So I searched,
And searched.
Every bottle becoming as empty as me.
Drunk now, not only off tequila, but on rage.
The alcohol came and went like so many shot glass friends.
You say cheers but no one knows joy.
Collide the glasses.
Tilt your head back and let the liquor flow down you like tears down your face.
Put the shot glass firmly against the table and then they are gone.
Shot glass friends are everywhere in LA.
I thought I would find the salvation at the bottom of a bottle
But tequila condemned me.

Millennial Love

So quick to fall into our screens but not into love.
More confident touching a keyboard than my skin.
Only willing to swipe left or right and never meet.
Following thousands of people with no direction.
But not following your own heart.

Don't Be Fooled

Don't let wings fool you.
They belong to both
Angels
And
Demons.

Greatest Fear

My greatest fear
Is that when I finally do find true love
Even that doesn't fill
The void in my heart.

Post Draft Day

The day after I was drafted I went looking for you
Where I knew I would find you.
That was one of the bitter things about being your son.
You were so close it must have been hard for you
To avoid me for a lifetime.
You let me into your girlfriends apartment,
None of your pictures on the wall,
You were a ghost in her life too.
I sat across from you at the kitchen table,
I don't think we've ever shared a meal together.
Looking at you for the first time in years I felt lied to.
You looked nothing like me. Warped by a life of deceit.
Lying put frown marks around your mouth and rotted your teeth.
A hat hid what little hair you had left, but not what little brains.
I spoke as little as possible. This was your chance,
Your last chance to apologize for everything you did wrong.
You were guilty of every crime, this was not a trial,
You had already been sentenced but I was left to serve your punishment.
You congratulated me, I was finally a professional.
I achieved something you sought but never achieved.
Maybe you hated me for it.
But for some reason none of that mattered, none of it.
Not the birthdays you missed. Not the nights I spent crying.
Not the days I waited at the door for you to come.
Not the lies you told strangers about my mother and me.
Not the new families you started after you declared me dead.
None of it.
It was as simple as two words.

Russell

The twenty something years, the million something lies,
All summed up into two words.
You never found those two.
Maybe you left them right where you left all the sons you
Wouldn't help become men.
Chosen to play in the National Football League,
And I still wasn't good enough to be chosen by you.
Too busy trying to explain when, where and why, instead of
focusing on how we fix things.
Too busy telling me your story instead of apologizing for being
The villain in mine.

Russell

The Prison Has Flowers

Russell

Blind

I remember the first time I saw you.

Not when I stumbled upon your Instagram and saw you in so many places with so little clothes.

I remember the first time I saw you.

Not when I picked you up from the airport. When we exchanged hellos, didn't touch but smiled at each other awkwardly. Trying to form sentences and questions that had meaning. Trying to find out if we had meaning.

I remember the first time I saw you.

Not when you pulled off my shirt. Kissed me on the neck, the chest, the hip. When you let me pull down your pants, push you up the bed, and turn you over.

I remember the first time I saw you.

The first time I really saw you. You snorting that line, kissing someone else, yelling at me making me think it was all my fault. I saw you for the first time with him, under him, filled by him. I really saw you and you
wanted so bad to hide from me you attempted murder by a broken heart.

I never want to see you again.

Begging

Staring to the sky on bent knees,
Asking God why he keeps waking me up.

Please let me rest.

Please let me die.

Missed Opportunity

I want that moment back.
I mean everything leading up to it was hell but I feel like I squandered that moment.
I kept asking you why you cheated?
How many times did you do it?
Was he better than me?
Was it worth it?
The only question my heart truly wanted to know was,
When did you stop loving me?
Why didn't I ask that question…
And could you have answered it?

Fate of Humanity

We sealed our fate.
We stopped looking to the skies to pray once we thought the stars fell and walked among us.
False idols have given claim to our souls,
Wandering through hell and we wander behind them like a lost herd.
Begging to be acknowledged by those who can't reward us.
To be honored by the dishonorable,
To find faith in sin.
We sealed our fate.
We stopped trying to love each other and started trying to hide ourselves.
We began to mimic and copy others who mimic and copy.
A history so long, twisted, and deprived we don't even know when it started.
God made men, and from that moment on, men have tried relentlessly to destroy
Those the Almighty himself loved as his children.
Such a low perception we have on humanity.
We lay with the serpent out of deep self loathing
Instead of interlacing fingers with the Father and letting him guide us.
We are Adam. We are Eve.
We sealed our fate.

Lovers Game

We took pride in coming up with new and sadistic ways to break each other.
Our games have no winners and we played until we lost score.

Vineyard Of Deceit

How many bottles of wine will it take for me to forget about you?
A bottle of red for the red heart you broke?
A bottle of white for the white lies you told?

Fragile

Didn't you know the dangers of planning your entire future
Around something
As fragile
As love?

Crying in The Rain

Loving you
Was like crying
In the rain.
I'm the only one who
Noticed.

Limbo

I've dropped to both knees at my bedside and begged God to take my life.
Too cowardly to kill myself
Yet too miserable to continue on.

A Page From Your Book

This wasn't as easy as you made it seem.
Sweat beaded down my brow as I let out cigarette smoke from a long drag.
I read and reread the manual left in your handwriting, looked over picture after picture like a step by step guide.

"Trust must be willingly given and there's no time table for this."

That's ok, I enjoy the long game. My twenties consumed by manipulations.

"Be there for everything, little or colossal until they began to depend on you. When they wake up they should reach for you out of habit even before they fully open their eyes. You become an extension of them."

I take a big gulp of ebony. Caffeine fueling a steady tapping of my left foot against marble. I ash my cigarette and wipe sleep from my eyes. This will be fun. God I need some fun.

"Every kiss needs to be precious."

I'm sorry I misread.

"Every kiss should feel precious. When your lips touch pleasure needs to burn through every memory and moment. When you aren't kissing, kissing you should be at the forefront of their mind."

I run my tongue over my bottom lip and feel it dry and cracked.

I need to take better care of my weapons.

"Now read closely. This is everything. Some people will think this is your goal but we both know it's just a byproduct; icing on the proverbial cake. Sex. SEX should be like GRAVITY. It should feel like it's the only thing holding them to this world. Without your sex they should feel as though they would float into the dark abyss,
forever alone, forever suffocating."

I didn't even realize I was on the edge of my seat.

"People think of breaking a heart like cracking open a skull, brutal, violent, gore, chaos. It can be, but where it should differ is in the hastefulness and sloppiness of it all. Breaking a heart should be slow, meticulous, thoughtful, and most of all enjoyable. It's more like skinning someone alive. Create random distance and mixed signals. Lie, badly, get caught and lie again. Only tell the truth when it's hurtful. Compliment everyone around them and focus only on their insecurities. Every argument make sure they end up apologizing. Make them doubt their sanity, and distrust their instincts. Talk to them less. Don't answer their calls or texts but when you're together always be on your phone. Enjoy every moment of this. I always do."

A laugh escapes me. A snicker maybe. I close my ex's book. It's a best seller.

Over Cliches

When did I grow to hate the phrase "I love you."
The three words make me cringe anytime someone throws around that hollow cliche.
"I love you" wasn't the confession I needed to hear.
Maybe you should have told me about the other men?
Or wait, maybe about the separate and secret bank account.
A confession would have been the abortion you had without my knowledge,
Our seed you murdered without my consent.
Now see those are confessions I would have gladly received.
But "I love you"
You have to come stronger than that.
But seriously, some transparency would have been appreciated.
We could have started anywhere.
We could have took turns.
You would have told me about your uncle's abuse.
I would have held you. Maybe even told you about mine.
At the least I would have shared about my stepfather's tragic death.
You would have cried for me.
I'm sure it wouldn't have been all bad.
You could tell me about your mother's tradition.
That every Sunday after church you go get ice cream together.
That she got rocky road and you always got green chocolate mint. I can see it now.
You smiling and reminiscing about a girl with braids, beads, a

crooked smile and the closest she ever felt to her judgmental southern baptist mother.
I would have held your hand right through the whole memory.
Then I would have told you about how my mom and I didn't have much but some mornings we would drive to a field right by the airport and watch the planes take off and land. We would guess where they came from,
pretend we knew where they were going and that we were on them.
You would have rubbed my back through the whole memory.
True confessions.
But instead you attempted to disappear
inside the relationship.
To use those three words to build a false sense of future.
I'd die for a confession over a cliche three times over.
But I guess it's not you it's me.

My Grass is Greener

Return from the other side.
My grass must finally be greener.
Tears have watered it since you left.

The Price to Play

Maybe I thought strapping on a helmet,
Buckling up some shoulder pads,
And lacing up a pair of cleats
Would give me value.

Maybe I thought brain damage was a poetic way to go.

Either way I played football for years and I loved to say it killed me.

Wonderland

Through the looking glass,
Alex stumbles to Wonderland.
The rabbit's time never lasts.
Maybe The Mad Hatter
Isn't all that mad.
Queen of hearts isn't hateful,
She's never been this sad.
Biggest heart in the kingdom,
Biggest chance of getting hurt.
Hate to love this complex tale,
Fairytale beyond the dirt.
Cheshire Cat disappears,
A trick I've seen many years.
Caterpillar smokes his pipe black
Cancer beyond his fear.
I'm never leaving or going back,
Wonderland has my soul.
Forget my life, forget the world,
I belong down the rabbit hole.

It's Always Winter in NYC

"Shouldn't writers move to New York City?"
I have to forgive them, of course they don't know. They don't know how that city has wronged me. What it's done to me. The frigid loneliness I feel surrounded by millions of strangers. The icy memories of being cheated on in Soho. The brisk chill of the hospital in Hell's kitchen that told Joe he had cancer. White snow everyone snorts just to live in Manhattan. Every memory I have in that city is arctic from Bronx to Staten Island.
I reply, "It's just too cold for me there."

My Tombstone

On my tombstone
Put the date I stopped writing.
That's when my soul left the earth.

Forgive Me Lord

Forgive me lord, for I have sinned.
I've turned my back and walked against thy wind.
Longest nights with no rest, painful days with no ends.
Demons and leaches disguised as my friends.
I pray to you Lord with my mind, body and soul.
Grant me merciful sleep which the devil has stole.

Aeronautics

I wonder if her
Angel Wings
Still fly
With all the stab wounds.

California King Bed

I think about you most when I'm about to try and sleep. When the night seems pitch black and my bed seems too big without you.

Toys

I don't see sexuality as two separate toy boxes.
I think it's a whole toy store
And we run wild
Trying things and breaking toys
Our parents will never know about.

Act Sober, Not Heartbroken

I submerge myself in liquor, drowning in it so I can remember,
Make sure you walk straight.
Make sure you don't slur your words too much.
Don't fall asleep at that club.
I thought if I had to remember such basic functions I wouldn't remember you.

Night Time Visitor

You grew on my heart like a tumor.
Our relationship malignant, and abnormal.
I kept filling you with every square inch of my soul,
I poured and poured pure love into you
And like the vapid abyss you were you devoured it all.
Remaining empty.
Where did it all go?
I discarded every watch I owned,
every calendar, every timer,
every measure of time I wasted on a false sense of us.
You're gone now but you visit me in my nightmares.

Digging for Love

I dug for love
Like it was a buried treasure.
Not knowing
It was a landmine.

The Village

It takes a village to raise a child.
My mother, being a single mother, needed that to be true more than anyone.
She worked herself to death to feed me.
She finished school to inspire me.
She listened when I spoke, and held me when I cried.
She just needed this village to protect me when she couldn't.
But villages, family or otherwise,
are riddled with assailants.
I didn't lose my innocence out in the world,
I lost it in that village.
That's one way to grow up real fast.

You Aren't Art

I fear writing about you
Using colorful words to paint your picture.
I do not intend to romanticize you.
What you did to me was not a poem.
It was abuse,
Neglect,
Hate,
Undeserving.
It was ugly.
I fear turning your sins into art.

Why Is Falling So Easy

Falling in love was so easy,
As it always is.
I didn't see you coming, you were an obstruction.
I tripped, stumbled, and despite my best efforts,
I came crashing down in love with you.
Falling in love was so easy.
Getting back up and brushing off the heartache was the challenge.

Natural Disaster

They will tell you tales of love.
It's up to you to know what's fact or fiction.
It's a chemical reaction in the brain, strong as a heroine addiction.
Love is just our survival instincts, our animalistic nature to procreate.
Love is this. Love is that. It ain't Love if you both aren't soulmates.

I think love is a force of nature, mysterious & strong.
Loving you was a natural disaster, but I wouldn't dare say it was wrong.

Cataclysm
Your words so passionate struck my tree of life,
Threatening to sever to the root.
Missing you was the earthquake cause by the tectonic plates.
My heart and brain violently rubbing together your pros and cons.
You swept me away. The tsunami of your sex rushed upon my shore,
Leaving devastation with no home to call my own but yours.
You became my shelter and then set us on wildfire with jealousy and rage.
Your love was gravity and no matter how hard, the cheating, the lies, the violence got
We were planted so firmly in the ground that we couldn't float away.
I thought you my shooting star and I wished upon you day and night.

Until I realized you were a meteor coming to crash through my ribs, into my heart, and leave a crater I would never fill.
When I laid with you rational thought was swept away by your tornado.
I had never been to Kansas but you were my Sorceress of OZ.
You were the end of days, the plague.
You were the reckoning, you were revelations.
You were genesis, I swear God said let there be light in that moment he crafted you.
Your love was so blinding I couldn't see.
So blinding I couldn't see the other men beyond your Sun.
So blinding I couldn't see you were the Moon controlling my tide.
So blinding I couldn't see you falling out of love with me fast and ferocious like a hole in the sky.
You opened up and let out all the rain at once or maybe that's just the water from my teary eyes.
If the body is 70 percent water I spent 80 percent crying over you.
You were a force of nature.
Maybe you were something else all together.
Nature and weather can be predicted but you could never be forecasted.

They will tell you tales of love, and I will tell them tales of you.
Only we know what's fact or fiction.
I've been stone cold sober from my, you addiction.
Somehow I survived the break. Writing stories you helped create.
Love is this. Love is that. But I'm still looking for my soulmate.

Inhume

Take me in.
Every night bury secrets
Beneath my skin.

New Journey, Old Soul

She held a hand she's held a million times
but my grasp was tighter.
Her thumbs ran across my knuckles and found scrapes and scars
that weren't there back when she knew me.
When she thought she knew me. Who was this man?
My face had been in her mind a thousand nights but now,
looking at me the glimmer in my eyes was new.
I had grown. Someone she knew but didn't.
Someone she cared for before and knew she could care for again.
A new adventure with a familiar spirit.
A new journey with an old soul.
Our new piece of forever.

Empty Garden

Amongst my garden, snakes do glide.
Serpents named Wrath, Greed, and Pride.
But of all the snakes I do not trust,
It's hard not to be charmed by that of Lust.
He drinks from the pond of love,
Relaxes underneath leaves of hope above.
Visitors fear his promiscuous bite.
No guest would stay through the night.
Finally I cornered him with my heartstone,
And bashed his skull in, tired of being alone.

Find Faith

It's hard to pray to a "benevolent" God
That's allowed the cruelest things you can imagine.

Mirror Mirror

Mirror mirror on the wall,
You're not the only thing that shatters when it falls.
I've fallen time and time again,
Somehow my pieces I seem to mend.
But mirror I'll never be the same
And heartbreak is the one to blame.

Necromancer

I'm a grave robber.
Yes, you died years ago,
But I exhume you with this pen,
Ritualize you in this ink,
And resurrect you in these pages.
Poetry is my necromancy.

My Flower Bed

As I grew older I began to obsess about nature.
I believe it was my body preparing to be called back home.
To be planted in the earth seven feet deep, and with no casket
The most stunning flowers would bloom.

Nightshade

I was hurt by my lover.
I told my hurt, he hurt another.
I was hurt by my dad.
I surpassed, but hurt grew sad.

I didn't let hurt see the sun.
Again and again I told him we were done.
But hurt grew each and every year.
Though I never acknowledged he was near.

Eventually I buried him, in my dirt soul.
And poison ivy sprouted from my heart whole.
Now I was toxic to all I saw,
Avoiding me now cardinal law.

Unfortunately two hearts did crash.
I told my lover of potential rash.
But of poison ivy she was not afraid.
When she didn't wake I knew it was nightshade.

Nature Needs Nurture

Don't plant seeds of
Love in my heart
If you're not
Going to tend to them
As they grow.

Need Me

I could drink myself dumb. Make you laugh and giggle as I dance with tequila on my breath.
I could drug myself dull. I'll be your steady rock, cry on my lithium shoulders and watch me not be moved.
I could hurt myself in secret. Smile to your face because I've made the pain physical and hid it on wrists you can't see.
I can be whoever you need me to be. I just want someone to need me to be.

Finish Line

I chased you
To what I thought
Was the end of the world.
Turns out,
It was just
The end of your love.

Sleepless

Of course I no longer sleep,
Every dream I've ever had I no longer want,
Every nightmare now living and walking amongst the day.

Your Grave Inside Me

You crawled inside me rotting and decrepit.
Nestling your head on my heart you sealed your eyes and died there.
Inside me now lay the most hideous parts of you.
The pungent odor of decaying dreams
You held throughout your childhood
Seeped through my pores.
The residue of your sexual prowess
Poured through my veins and ran my temperature to a boil.
Your flesh was eaten slowly by my insecurities.
Your organs melted and pooled inside my chest.
Your bones left a skeletal graveyard right by my heart.

What Comes Natural

To be around so many people striving,
Dreaming,
Achieving,
And yet you're doing nothing.
It's unnatural.
To have wings and watch so many soar around you,
While you stay grounded is unnatural.
Jump,
Leap,
And fly!
Your greatness is natural.

Home

They say home is where the heart is but I've been
Evicted,
Homeless
And in shelters for awhile now.

Men and Boys

In those days
Native men, the original men,
Welcomed intruders as privileged guests.
The intruders loaded that privilege into guns.
They had no intentions of staying guests.

In these days
Young men, sometimes boys,
Grant fearful men shields to serve and protect.
Fearful men disregard the shield to use the gun.
They had no intentions of protecting us.

Be A Man

Through adolescence
I had to fit all my emotions
Into the simple phrase
"Man up."

The Free Man's Repletion

My History, My Future

100 yards and a pigskin.
Slaves to circumstance and prejudice.
Newly freed from the ghetto.
Reparation isn't resurrection.
I'll always be this color,
You'll always remind me of that.
What do you put
On the tombstone of a teenager?
Do you think we vanish back into
The abyss of our skin color.
Maybe we buy chains and gold so flashy
You see us as human.
Or maybe I just want you to stop clutching
Your purse cause I can afford better.
I'm not convinced you hate me.
If you did you wouldn't steal everything about me.
Maybe you fear me, but I'm not sure
You think about anything but yourself.
Maybe you hate yourself?
Fear what you are capable of.
Maybe you think the end is
An abyss as dark as my skin
And it will call you home.
Will you put murderer on your tombstone?
Child killer maybe?
Do you think making Jesus white
Made you holy?
If we were all made in his image
Where did you find such privilege?

Forgiving isn't forgetting.
Truly freed from oppressive constructs.

Slaves only to my desires and my lovers.
40 acres and a mule.

Masculine Overdose

It was a toxic dose of masculinity
They injected into every part of my life.
I was denied the natural chemistry of emotions.
The coroner report read, "Death by alexithymia."

The Border Between

I truly began to understand how fragile the border
between love and hate is when
Every small indiscretion seemed like an
Egregious attempt at my life.
You were slowly and subtly killing me.

Blacksmith

As iron sharpens iron
Love sharpens lust.
Cut me down the center
With swords we spent
All night forging.

Striking Oil

I spent years digging into you in hopes of striking gold,
Instead your black emptiness spouted to the top like oil.
I drowned in it.
Gagging on the thick sad liquid of your hypocrisy.
Clawing at my own neck
For a moment of love.

The Boy and The Demon

I fed the boy to the demon.
Crown first the way his mother bore him.
The monster was more teeth than jaw.
Yellow eyes, slit, like that of a serpent.
Broad nose, pointed ears.
He danced on four legs like that of a stead.
Claws the size of pitch forks.
Two sets of wings appropriate his spine.
Scales dripping with black sludge.
The demon was mute but I knew his hunger.
He craved what only I could give, what I always gave.
Carnal desire beckoning , without forewarning.
He stayed as long as he liked, my life his dominion.
The boy however was my claim.
Nameless, young, and beautiful.
Eyes that tell all.
Hands that fumble with every touch.
Bountiful curls atop his head.
Rambunctious soul of his.
But the boy must have known he was my sacrifice.
Why else would I keep him?
I was much stronger than the boy. Strong in the sense that others valued.
I was high functioning and non threatening.
Always visible but just out of reach.
Without me the boy was vulnerable.
With him so was I.
He was hysterical laughter or gut wrenching screams, never anything in between.
The world so small through his lens, everything so bright in his

mind's eye.
A type of rose colored frame, had the boy so mesmerized
he hardly saw but always empathized.
He felt more than he could handle. The demon ate more than he
could stomach. After gnawing on the boy for what seemed like
lifetimes, he regurgitates his meal.
Spitting the boy out broken, but intact, right at my feet.
He lay on his back the way his father buried him.
I succumb to our ritual
Apologizing and promising to never forsake
the boy again.
He is afflicted with a naive heart and forgiving soul.
In no time at all, he forgets and I wait.
I will feed the boy to the demon again.

Hour Glass

Can anyone stop him.
Time is killing everyone I love.
Hour glass serial murder.

Good Morning

The Sun soared over the horizon.
My eyes peered open,
My breath quickened,
My hand reached out...

And felt you.
Good morning indeed.

Give And Take

Pleasure and trust came in a bundle like a his and hers gift
straight from glory.
Skin on skin with no end in sight.
Push and pull, flying and falling.
I wanted it all,
Her soft kisses and sweet whispers.
I ventured to go deeper than anyone and bury my love
dead center in her being.
She had all of me and she clawed at my back for more.
She was the picture of transparency.
She gave me calm, a home safer
than anyone I had known.
She opened up for me and bloomed
as the flower of ecstasy grew,
Rooted in care and compassion,
Watered by time and trust.
Give and take.
Give me love.
Take my love.
Love on love with no end in sight.

Commitment on The Shores

Please love, take my hand.
Lace your fingers, your dreams with mine, and I will hold on tight.
Let's walk just you and I, with our toes in the sand,
The tide of endless possibilities rising
and falling underneath us.
Every speck of dust containing its own universe.
We are the destroyers of worlds.
I will walk with you until my knees shake from the weight of your hurt,
Until my feet are raw on the bottom like my heart.
I will walk with you until you can't walk anymore,
And as true suitors do I will carry you.
I will carry you down the shore of forever. Until I can't bare to stand upright any longer,
And as your true paramour I will lay with you.
I will lay with you here on the sand, atop a million little worlds, until the same waves that brought us comfort sweep us away.
And I, your inamorato will drown with you.
I will drown with you perpetually in the depths of dreams and space.
I swear to you,
I will hold your hand from the beginning of time until the end of oblivion.

Illumination

Her past lovers were shades and shadows.
I sought to be nothing more than extra wattage for her light.
Her soul illuminated my world.

Reveled

I thought love would bring out the best in me.
But it reveled me.
The ugliest darkest parts of me were exposed
for one person to judge.

Rules Don't Rule Me

It's the same game.
I thought I knew all the rules.
But when did football dictate
Who I prayed to?
Who I stood up for?
Who I aligned myself with?
Who I loved?
When did the rules
Stop trying to regulate
And started trying to redefine?

Teacher's Mistake

We teach the people in our lives how to love us.
But if every one of my students have failed,
Then the incompetent one must be the teacher.

Love Chose Us

I always thought love was deliberate.
A choice being made.
A decision.
But now,
I don't even remember when I started
To need you.

Location

The past doesn't matter.
She left me
Right where you could find me.

Wounds or Wings

It was the most intimate act I had ever agreed to.
I took off my shirt and laid face down on her queen bed. She straddled me, trapped me in my most vulnerable state.
Kisses trailed along my neck, a low moan escaped my lips. Gently, slowly, and all at once, she began to work her hands through the knots of my lower back.
Immeasurable fear sprung free from the Jack in the heart box. Yet, I used all my might to stuff the springs back from where they came. I clenched my eyes shut as hard as possible. I was afraid of what she would see and touch.
All the wounds of past lovers and demons who owned a small stab mark in my back. I was positive the sheer number of people whom I let penetrate my heart would repulse her.
She found her rhythm and continued a specific trail along both my sides. It seemed like hours before she finally spoke.
"I can tell you used to have wings here."
The scars are jagged, wild, and blind. The patterns of them would insinuate they were self-inflicted.
I forced air into my lungs. I couldn't reply just then. I just kept reminding myself to breath.
She continued, "Who talked you into mutilating yourself?"
She stopped moving her hands, then, she needed an answer. I balled up the sheet underneath me with clenched fists and forced myself to speak,
"They didn't talk me into anything. I gave my wings to them, and in the end, they used them to fly away."
I wasn't sure what she was thinking. All I could hear was my labored and forced breath.
Finally she answered,

"Then I will give you one of mine. Sharing the most beautiful part of myself but grounding myself to you as well. Let me heal you."
I cried all night and she never stopped rubbing my back and kissing my neck.

School Project

Write a list of your 10 favorite people of all time...

Then ask yourself, why you don't make it on your own list?

Know The Difference

I think it's important for everyone to understand
That missing something
Isn't always the same thing
As wanting it back.

Unholy Trinity

Sinner was an understatement.
I was devoted to an unholy trinity,
Of sex, drugs,
And love.

Heartstrings

I tried to write
Without music.
To listen to my thoughts,
But you're the only
Tune my mind sings.
Your love is that song
Stuck in my head.

Witchcraft

She danced the way
I wrote poems,
Spellbound
And compulsive.

Love Is My Flower

Love makes you sprout from the ground,
Open up to the sun,
And share the perfume of infatuation
With the world.

Americano

I love coffee shops with
Strong espressos,
Reliable WiFi,
And an endless tap
Of free flowing ideas.

Football is Not War

Do not cry, mother, for football is not war.
We do not carry arms against the less fortunate,
Or shoot amongst the crowd.
And the divided sides are not nations,
But boys that thought playing a game
Made them men.
Do not cry, mother.
Football is not war.

Yelling men, beer overflowing, we enter the arena.
Rage filled eyes, black war paint, but football is not war.
These boys were made to break but they've been bending their whole lives.
Glory awaits for those whose colors stand high in blood tides.
Fight for the man whose branded you,
Your helmet his homage.
Do not cry mother.
Football is not war.

Do not cry, mother, for football is not war.
Because I chose this path, it averted me from the slums.
Sweat filled my eyes better than tears.
A belly of blood was full at last.
Grass fields I wished I could die on,
Over the streets that claimed young lives.
Do not cry mother.
Football is not war.

Do not cry, mother, for football is not war.
There's whistles, balls, and bright colors,
It's an arcade game I swear.

Forget the diagnoses, broken bones, and drug abuse.
CTE is not PTSD,
And I'd choose this half life over and over again.
Do not cry mother.
Football is not war.

Mother whose heart stops when I crumble.
Who wonders, maybe this time I'll stay down.
Do not cry mother.
Football is not war.

7 Billion Artists

It's remarkable,
The different mediums
God gives us
To express his light
And illustrate his love.

We live in the same world
Yet interpret and perceive its beauty
7 billion ways.
Each expression just as stunning as the next.

Prison or Passion

Similar to the relief from a good cry.
The prism of colors after the storm.
The derivative of pain can be beauty.
Sometimes your purpose lies
Amongst the rubble of your dreams.
Adversity, sorrow, misfortune,
Don't let it imprison you.
See the prosperity after the trial,
Be invigorated by the challenges.
You will find that this prison
In fact bred your passion.
For me the same ache
That moves my pen,
Liberates my heart.

Before You

Loving you is the best amnesia.
Every kiss clouds my worst memories.
Every touch fills that empty void.
And when we lay together
The past disappears and there was never anything
before loving you.

Lights Shine Brightest At Night

There in the infinite view of the ocean,
The endless blue of the sky,
The constant warmth of the sun,
She took great pleasure in the realization of how small she was.
How minuscule each problem
And obstacle she faced unquestionably was.
Every evil in this world was minimal
Compared to the beauty in front of her,
The beauty within her.

I love you mother.

Solemnly Swear

I cherish the
Traumatized
Boy
I used to be.
I vow
To grow
Into the man
That would have protected him.

Lovers List

I could care less
Who you've loved.
As long as
You add me to the list.

Boy With Feelings

Yes I am a boy, they told me so.
I'm not pretty but handsome, I wear blue in photos,
But when my heart starts to hurt,
They do not want to hear it.
I tell them
It's in the ocean of my eyes,
The emptiness of my arms,
The gasp between my cries,
The quiver from your harms.
I am a boy,
they told me so.
Boy with feelings,
Let me grow.

I have to stand up straight
I can never show fear,
And to other boys,
Intimidated, poised, or
Subordinate they know to stay clear.
We pretend to like cigs, drink beer,
We are auto-tuned to this gear.
But I tell them,
It's in the shake of my knees,
The ache to be touched,
The jealousy of never having,
A reliable crutch.
I am a boy,
They told me so.
Boy with feelings,
Let me grow.

Other boys have asked
Why boy, do you want to feel?
They neglect the heart,
Blinded from love's art.
More demon than men,
Taught to destroy instead of build.
Repression is strength, they think that's real.
But I tell them,
It's in the nurture of a woman.
It's in protecting without supressing.
The beauty in vulnerability,
Not knowing and sometimes guessing.
I am a boy,
They told me so.
Boy with feelings,
Let me grow.

Finally you realize
We were meant to be whole.
We are more then masculine anger.
Be loving, soft, and still reach our goal.
Witness my emotions,
Dive in the depth of my soul.
I tell them,
I can use my mind,
Brute force is my last weapon.
I can speak soft and be heard,
Not demeaned if my women step in.
Cause I am a man,
I told them so.
Man with feelings,
Watch me grow.

Bring Souls Together

Vessels for our soul,
Ships held by the same anchor.
The crash of two shooting stars,
Two different trajectories,
Two ends of an endless multiverse,
But somehow collided.

Suffocation kisses stealing breath away.
Never knowing earthly names only divine resonance.
Never looking eye to eye but drowning in the pool of existence.
Lips don't touch, fates do.
Fates marry,
Destinies honeymoon,
And love procreates and surpasses us
As offspring that will never cease.

Souls for our vessels,
Shrines that honor not life, but affection.
Worship and praise the religion of love,
The one true God immortal.
Long live the beautiful vessel that die.
Vessels, ships, stars,
Who bring souls together.

Grey & Gold

She could never just enjoy the storm.
She was always waiting for the rainbow.
She said it was art, colors painted across sky canvas.

Red was how she loved me. That's what she told me, hot and passionate.

Blue reminded her of me. Calm and cool, oceanic steadiness, waterfall power.

Green she used to describe herself. Green with envy when any other girl had my attention.
That wasn't often if ever.

Purple was her garden she often talked about starting.
She longed for endless country hills, and flowers.
I did not know the name of every flower, only they were not as beautiful as she.

Orange were the sunrises we set alarms to wake up and watch hand in hand.

By the time she got to yellow I must admit I wasn't listening much.
I was too busy distracting her with a trail of kisses on her neck.
Maybe she never got to yellow at all.

She loved the rainbow and she was my pot of gold at the end of it.
I'm not sure she ever knew, but I didn't care much for the rainbow.

I loved the storm. You see my favorite color was grey.

Grey made the sky dark enough for us to get closer,
But bright enough that nothing was hidden from me.

Thunder is grey as well.
Loud so she grabs me until her knuckles turn white.
Patient enough for me to space out tender touches in the black.

We don't have to go outside to our prim, proper, clean white lives.
It's still early so we won't slip into dark black sleep.
No, it's grey.
Somewhere between living and sleeping, that's where love is.

Grey storms are the white lies of, "Baby it's too dangerous to leave,"
And the black intentions of trapping you in this moment of eternity with me.
Let the lightning strike.
Strike my heart.
Strike my love.
Strike us down right here, right now.
Let me die in grey with you.

My pot of gold at the end of the rainbow.

Zeyna

She put on mascara
Like war paint
But she had already
Conquered my rebellious heart.

Give Me a Ring

If you give me a ring
I'll put it through a chain,
And let it hang over the organ
That beats your name sixty times a minute.
I don't want to stuff my hands in my pockets
Accidentally hiding you.
Blue collar hands calloused from labor.
Our love is leisure.

Give me a ring.
I'll put it through a chain.
If one day you want it back
You can hang me from it and
Bury me where you stopped loving me.

Mix and Match

I always seem to
Get to the bottom of the bottle
Before getting to the bottom of my problems.
Maybe problems are endless
And bottles should be made infinite.

World Travelers

My mother and I used to travel the world together.
I was no younger than twelve and in one day
We would circle the globe twice.
I longed for our travel days, I called them our world tours.
We would pack pretty light but bring all the snacks
We could carry. A day of travel required snacks.
Mother would ask me to bring a blanket
But I often forget so she brought two just in case.
She would also bring a book, and I made sure
To talk so much she never cracked it open.
Our seats were better than first class,
We reclined back as far as we wanted,
And listened to music softly but without headphones.
It was noon on Sunday so we had plenty of flights to catch.
In a blink the first flight takes off.
Before my mind could wake up and my imagination could stretch my mother speaks,
"Paris. Paris. Don't you see the Eiffel? Don't you smell the pastries?
Isn't it lovely in this cafe? Waiter could you bring me a coffee and a juice for the boy?"
I spoke up,
"But mother, it's a vacation. Can't I have a coffee just this once?"
She pondered for a moment, just enough to make me worry.
"Good sir a cup of coffee for the boy as well, actually can you bring us the whole pot?"
My grin was ear to ear and my laugh filled the car.
Mother shrugged,
"When in Rome." She said.
At that moment another plane takes off and I spring into action pointing.

"Rome! Mother, Rome! Isn't it lovely? The statues of the Gods. The Colloseum. The gladiators, mother the gladiators they are fighting just for us!"
Mother smiled and asked,
"Who will win?"
To which I answered,
"Tetraites will win. He has a mother at home waiting for him. He promised her he would return."
Before it was noticeable my mother wipes a tear from her eye and gives me a kiss.
The whole day we watched planes take off and
They took our imaginations with them.

Hit Snooze

I hate when you set alarms
That scream at you
To leave me.

Past Lives

I've got some scars
I'm trying to hide.
I've got past lives
That haven't died.

Lust

Lost
Under
Sex
Trance.

Ultraviolet Jealousy

Sleep still in my eyes,
The taste of you on my tongue,
Our limbs intertwined to no end.
Sun peaked through our window
Enviously hoping to witness,
The spectacle Moon
Gossiped about us performing all night.

Morning Star and Lady Luna

The Morning Star rose and burned until I lost count.
He needed no permissions to continue his path,
His constant search for his lover.
His lady, The Moon loved to be chased,
Maybe more than she loved to be loved.
I watched him chase her.
I watched her toy with him.
He hopes it's a love story.
She thinks it's a game.
I just hope it never ends. Not even an eclipse.

DUI

Left hand on the steering wheel,
Right hand on your thigh,
Just as all my favorite hip hop songs instructed.
Sped around every turn just so I could hear you laugh.
Each speed bump I hit too hard, and let my hand explore your skin.
All the traffic lights, both yellow and red,
I stopped to look into your eyes
And press my lips against yours.
Driving while under your influence.

Side by Side

On the football field, we stood side by side.
We tackled all our problems stride for stride.
We became roommates, I partied you abstained.
I drowned myself in liquor, you healed me when I was pained.
Neither of us had a father, but you helped raise me.
More man at 26 than most, all who knew you would agree.
I made it to the big leagues, you married one of my dearest friends.
Our lives didn't start as a fairytale, but I think that it contends.
I was the best man at your wedding, the greatest honor of my life.
I smile just thinking about dancing with you and your wife.
Your smile was always big, but it filled the room that day.
And everyday you said the words Mrs. Gilliam, I knew that smile was here to stay.
2017 the three of us went to New York City.
It was cold as heck, but it was your birthday and pure snow is kinda pretty.
We went to some sights, dove into some bars, O the spectacles we witnessed.
Until the next morning came, and you couldn't walk. First signs of the sickness.
The following year is gruesome for me to recall, I couldn't imagine how it was for you to endure.
The sickness wrapping around your spine, crushing your body at its core.
In no time at all, you couldn't walk. Your other motor functions dwindling fast.
It became apparent at 26, you would breath your last.
On the hospital bed, we laid side by side.
We spoke farewells, and cried and cried and cried.

Joe

Think of all the days we had left.
The memories that are now just dreams
That will only be dreams.

I laugh about the best man speech
You would have given at my wedding.
I already know the jokes you would
Have told, and the stories you would
Keep because they aren't appropriate
For a love story.

I smile when I think about the guy trips.
Me, you, and Devin arguing against
Whatever Antione was saying.
You and Rico talking about the married life
While I swore I didn't wanna have kids.
Where would we have gone?

I cry a bit when I think about having a son.
You know he's gonna be named after you.
He's going to be named after the man
I want him to grow into.
The best human I've ever met.

Think of all the days you had left.

Talk to me.

Listen to me, we are going to have this talk.
I don't know what you could be busy up there doing?
I don't know if you and God have some kind of running joke, but no ones fucking laughing.
It wasn't funny when you got cancer.
It wasn't hysterical when you couldn't walk anymore.
I don't remember us laughing when you lost all your hair.
The chemo wasn't a punchline, the endless hospital visits weren't a witty twist.
Just stop it, it's not fucking funny.

Listen to me, we are going to have this talk.
It's not going to be one sided either.
It's not going to be like all the other talks we've had since you left me.
It's not going to be me screaming into a pillow, me crying pulled over on the side of the road.
I'm not calling you anymore, just to get your voicemail, to finally hear you say your name, and me leave a message you will never return.
No more drunken curse filled rants that lose reason.

Listen to me Joseph we are going to have this talk.
We are going to have this talk because it hurts when I breath.
Because I forget every morning and when I wake up its like losing you again.
Because I never got a chance to say the right things at the right times.
We are going to talk because you were 26 and we had a lifetime of conversations left to be had.
You are going to fucking talk to me.

Russell

You know I force myself to sleep. I do.
I take sleeping pills, I drink alcohol, I workout until my body physically shuts down.
Someone told me once your loved ones will visit you in your dreams.
So I leave my mind light on, and my welcome heart mat at the dream door.
I don't know if you and God have some running joke, but no ones fucking laughing.
It wasn't funny when he took you from me.
All I'm asking for is a visit in my dreams.
Listen to me, we are going to have this talk.

Magnet

The words they
Come to me.
More frequent than dreams.
More tortured than nightmare.
The poems they
Come to me.

Just say it

If you love someone,
Tell them.
Just because your voice will crack,
Doesn't mean your heart will break.

Guillotine Grander

I stuck my neck out, as far as my shoulders would let me.
Clamped and clasped in place under the weight
of his sharp edge rage.
The reflection of my terror danced off the blade.
All silent but the crows.
All watching but the children.
Fear begged me to close my eyes but I denied it. They would be closed soon enough and I was going to drink in every last bit of the end.
Father needed no black mask for me to call him executioner.
The basket lay underneath me waiting to claim thy head.
Liquor his courage, he pulled the rope of fate and the guillotine severed the air in half as it rushed to and through my nape.
Forsaken in the courtyard for all the abused to witness.

Last Russell Standing

I would not say that I have forgiven my father.
What I will say is,
I've become more gracious with myself.
I don't blame the little boy for wanting his father.
I'm not mad at the teenager who lashed out and didn't know why.
I am no longer disgusted by the young man who didn't know how a man should love.
I forgive myself. I do it every day.
It felt like nothing I could do would hurt you
So instead I hurt me.
My life isn't about you.
It shouldn't have been to begin with.
I'll never try to make it that way again.

Malibu Nights

Laying on the beach gazing at the moon I find myself at peace.
No one to cater to, nothing to worry about.
The vibrations of the world go quiet.
I can start to hear my heart beat,
A calm,
Simplistic rhythm.
A sense of self takes shape with striking detail, and my dreams start to awaken.
Longing for a warmth that can withhold a simple truth,
Coming up short relying on love and companionship.
Alone listening, moonlight flooding the sand, a
realization of clarity.
I am, who needs me.
The world needs me.
To find the warmth, I needed only to look within.
Focus on the dreams and talents given,
let your happiness lead you.
To matter is to exist.
Live to learn,
Forgive and you'll forget.
Experience the world and all facets of its gifts.
Be alone and be happy.
Be with friends and spread vibes.
Find that joy and give it right back.

Malibu Mirror

In the mirror of the ocean
We are all angels in the sky.

NFL

My glass slipper had cleats attached.
I didn't have seven dwarfs but seven coaches
who never let me sleep.
Excalibur made of pigskin,
Camelot was a distant promise of greater lands,
Through the enchanted forest far away from the ghetto.

There were Villains. But my archenemies shared my name.
Comrades, warriors, brothers, and friends
that died along the way.
I think there's a princess but I haven't found a tower high
enough to hold my soulmate.
I fight dragons who breath
depression, anxiety, and racism.
Waking atop of bones of freedom
fighting knights who came before me.

Happily ever after isn't death.
It's riding off in the sunset with your dreams in hand.
It's where your true life begins.
For me it was making it in the NFL.

National Fairytale League.

Free Man

I will not be your prisoner.
Circumstance is no warden of mine.
I am a free man.
Free to love and heal as I see fit.

Poets Immortal

Poetry is my favorite form of expression,
A painting in one stroke.
It's a picture with perfect resolution.
Your favorite book you can read again and again.
It's the climax of every story.
Poetry is the purest part of life,
Without death.
Immortality.

Me

Scribbler of poems
Protector of the innocent
Damaged lover
Abandonment survivor
Second hand cancer casualty
Novice iPhone photo junky
Footbrawler
Ninja Fanatic
Sneaker Head
Sober Rasta
Church and therapist advocate.

Now You Know

There is too much of me across these pages.
Every line,
Every verse,
Every poem,
No matter the subject is a portrait of me.
The topic of the poem is merely
A gateway,
A looking glass,
A telescope,
Into the vastness of my soul.
These poems do not reveal
Who are angels,
And who are demons,
They reveal me.
To read this is to know me.
Maybe closer than those who have known me my whole life.
Maybe more than those whose names
I will utter in my last breath.
Now you know me as God does.
All my hopes, dreams, and wishes.
Now you know me as Satan does.
All my desires, insecurities, and SINS.

Russell

Copyright © 2019 R.K. Russell.

All rights reserved. This book or any portion thereof may not be reproduced or used in any manner whatsoever without the express written permission of the publisher except for the use of brief quotations in a book review.

First printing, 2019.

Jack Wild Publishing LLC

www.rkrelentless.com

www.jackwildpublishing.com

Printed in Great Britain
by Amazon